McGraw-Hill's
FRENCH
ILLUSTRATED
DICTIONARY

New York   Chicago   San Francisco   Lisbon   London   Madrid   Mexico City
Milan   New Delhi   San Juan   Seoul   Singapore   Sydney   Toronto

1 2 3 4 5 6 7 8 9 10   CTP/SGC   1 0 9 8 7 6 5 4 3

ISBN   978-0-07-181730-1 (book and CD set)
MHID   0-07-181730-1   (book and CD set)

ISBN   978-0-07-181728-8 (book for set)
MHID   0-07-181728-X   (book for set)

Library of Congress Control Number 2013930861

MP3 Disk

The accompanying disk contains MP3 recordings of all terms presented in this dictionary. These files can be played on your computer and loaded onto your MP3 player.

To load MP3 files on your iPod or similar MP3 player:

1. Open iTunes on your computer.
2. Insert the disk into your computer and open via My Computer.
3. Drag the folder "French Dict MP3s" into the Music Library in the iTunes menu.
4. Sync your iPod with iTunes and eject the iPod.
5. Locate the recordings on your iPod by following this path:

   Main menu: Menu
   Music menu: Artists
   Artist menu: French Illustrated Dictionary

6. If you experience difficulties, check the Read Me file on the disk.

McGraw-Hill products are available at special quantity discounts to use as premiums and sales promotions or for use in corporate training programs. To contact a representative, please e-mail us at bulksales@mcgraw-hill.com.

This book is printed on acid-free paper.

Contents

How to Use This Book

It is suggested that you listen to the audio recordings when using this book. It will make your learning more efficient.

Category title
shown in English

Unit title including English and French

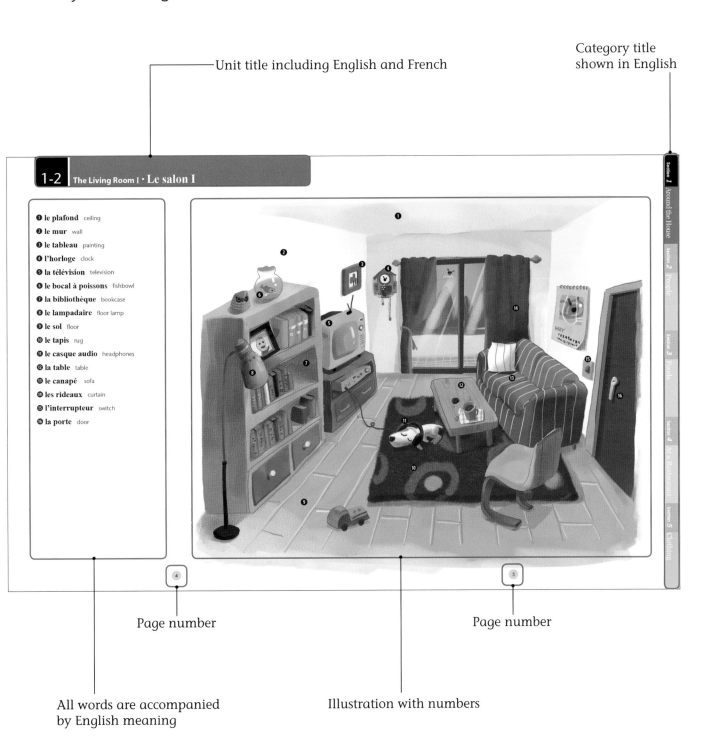

1-2 The Living Room I · Le salon I

❶ le plafond ceiling
❷ le mur wall
❸ le tableau painting
❹ l'horloge clock
❺ la télévision television
❻ le bocal à poissons fishbowl
❼ la bibliothèque bookcase
❽ le lampadaire floor lamp
❾ le sol floor
❿ le tapis rug
⓫ le casque audio headphones
⓬ la table table
⓭ le canapé sofa
⓮ les rideaux curtain
⓯ l'interrupteur switch
⓰ la porte door

Section 1 Around the House
Section 2 People
Section 3 Foods
Section 4 At a Restaurant
Section 5 Clothing

Page number 4

Page number 5

All words are accompanied
by English meaning

Illustration with numbers

❶ **l'immeuble** building

❷ **la fenêtre** window

❸ **la piscine** swimming pool

❹ **la porte principale** main door

❺ **le gardien** doorman

❻ **l'appartement** apartment

❼ le balcon balcony

❽ le toit-terrasse top floor

❾ l'escalier stair

❿ le garage garage

⓫ la cour yard

⓬ la boîte aux lettres mailbox

3

❶ le plafond ceiling

❷ le mur wall

❸ le tableau painting

❹ l'horloge clock

❺ la télévision television

❻ le bocal à poissons fishbowl

❼ la bibliothèque bookcase

❽ le lampadaire floor lamp

❾ le sol floor

❿ le tapis rug

⓫ le casque audio headphones

⓬ la table table

⓭ le canapé sofa

⓮ les rideaux curtain

⓯ l'interrupteur switch

⓰ la porte door

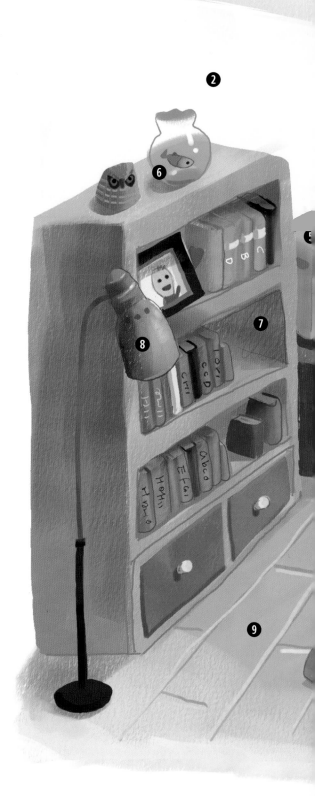

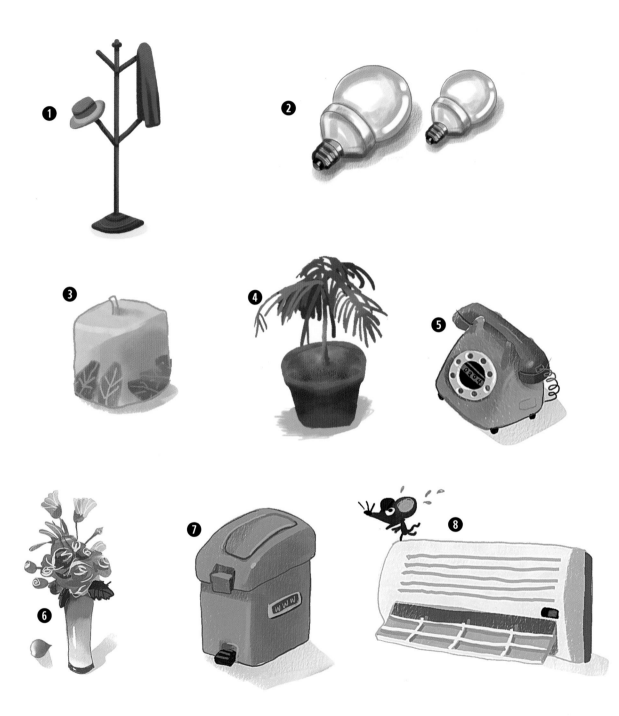

❶ le porte-manteau coatrack

❷ l'ampoule light bulb

❸ la bougie candle

❹ la plante en pot potted plant

❺ le téléphone telephone

❻ le vase vase

❼ la poubelle trash can

❽ le climatiseur air conditioner

❾ le chauffage   heater

❿ le ventilateur   fan

⓫ la chaîne Hi-fi   stereo

⓬ le lecteur de DVD   DVD player

⓭ la télécommande   remote control

⓮ l'aspirateur   vacuum cleaner

⓯ le répondeur téléphonique
answering machine

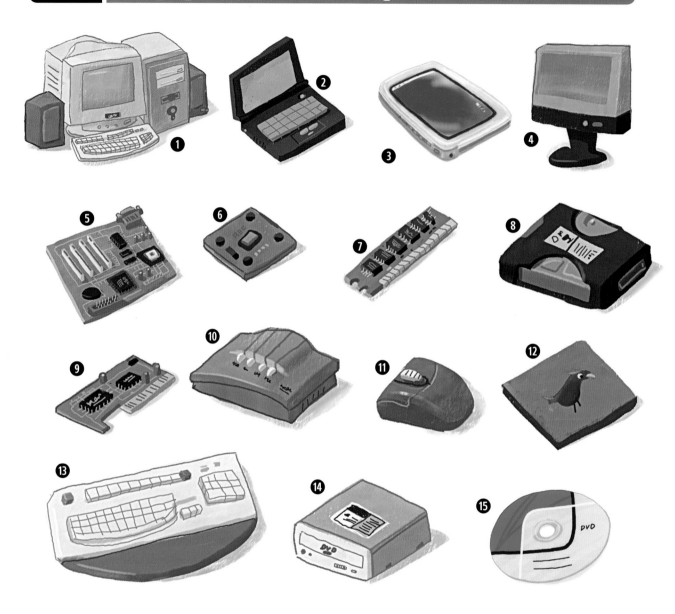

❶ **l'ordinateur de bureau**
desktop computer

❷ **l'ordinateur portable / le netbook**
laptop computer

❸ **la tablette numérique** tablet PC

❹ **l'écran à cristaux liquides**
LCD monitor

❺ **la carte mère** motherboard

❻ **l'unité centrale** CPU

❼ **la mémoire** RAM

❽ **le disque dur** hard disk

❾ **la carte réseau** network adapter card

❿ **le modem** modem

⓫ **la souris** mouse

⓬ **le tapis de souris** mouse pad

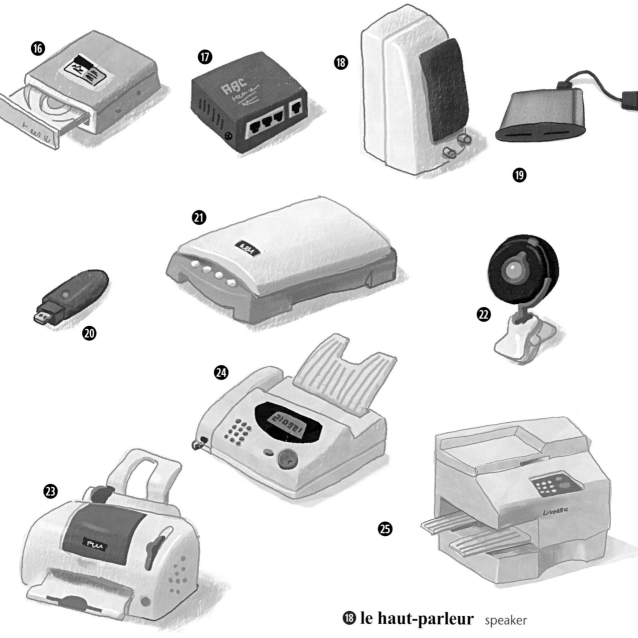

⑱ le haut-parleur speaker

⑲ le lecteur de cartes card reader

⑬ le clavier keyboard

⑳ la clé USB flash drive

⑭ le lecteur de DVD
DVD-ROM drive

㉑ le scanner scanner

⑮ le DVD DVD

㉒ la webcam webcam

⑯ le graveur de disque CD burner

㉓ l'imprimante printer

⑰ le concentrateur Ethernet / le bus Ethernet hub

㉔ le fax fax machine

㉕ la photocopieuse photocopier

❶ **le carreau**   tile

❷ **l'étagère**   shelf

❸ **le miroir**   mirror

❹ **la prise**   socket

❺ **la serviette de bain**   bath towel

❻ **la serviette de toilette**   towel

❼ **le lavabo**   sink

❽ **le robinet**   faucet

❾ **le papier hygiénique /
   le papier toilettes**   toilet paper

❿ **le réservoir d'eau**   toilet tank

⓫ **la cuvette**   toilet

⓬ **le trou d'écoulement**   drain

⓭ **le tapis de salle de bains**   bath mat

⓮ **le rideau de douche**   shower curtain

⓯ **le pommeau de douche**   showerhead

⓰ **la baignoire**   bathtub

❶ le rasoir razor

❷ le rasoir électrique electric razor

❸ la crème pour les mains hand cream

❹ le nettoyant facial wash

❺ le shampoing shampoo

❻ l'après-shampoing conditioner

❼ le gel douche shower gel

❽ le savon soap

❾ la crème pour le corps body lotion

❿ la brosse à dents toothbrush

⓫ le dentifrice toothpaste

⓬ le sèche-cheveux blow-dryer

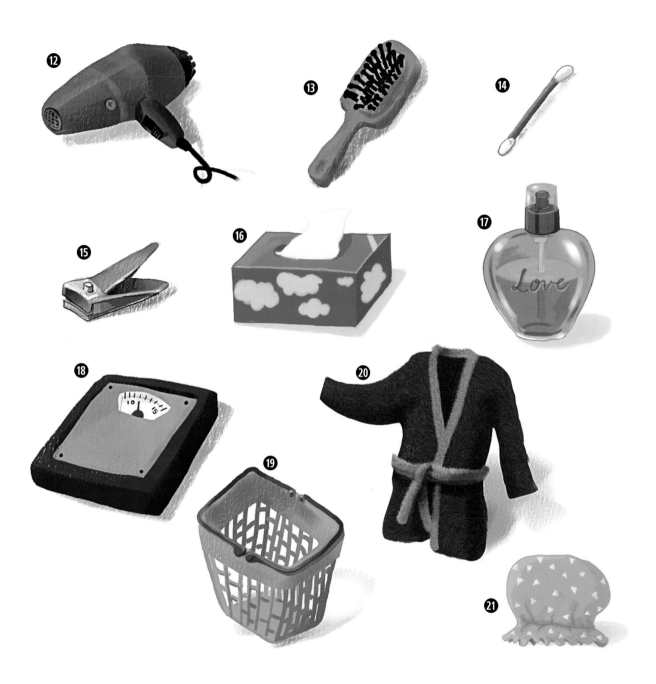

⑬ **la brosse à cheveux** hairbrush

⑭ **le coton tige** cotton swab

⑮ **le coupe-ongles** nail clipper

⑯ **le mouchoir** facial tissues

⑰ **le parfum** perfume

⑱ **la balance** scale

⑲ **le panier à linge** laundry basket

⑳ **le peignoir** bathrobe

㉑ **le bonnet de bain** shower cap

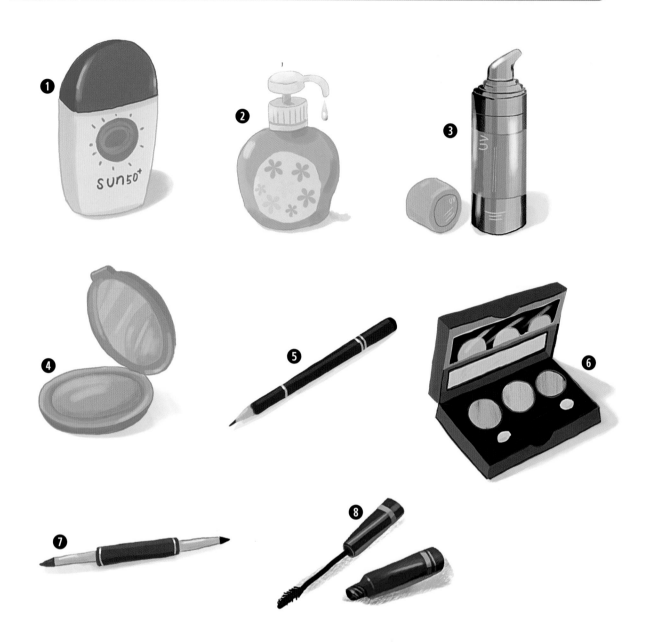

❶ la crème solaire sunscreen

❷ la crème hydratante moisturizer

❸ le fond de teint foundation

❹ le fond de teint compact
compact foundation

❺ le crayon à sourcils eyebrow pencil

❻ le fard à paupières eye shadow

❼ l'eye-liner eyeliner

❽ le mascara mascara

❾ le recourbe-cils eyelash curler

❿ le fard à joues blush

⓫ le pinceau brush

⓬ le rouge à lèvres lipstick

⓭ le vernis à ongles nail polish

⓮ le démaquillant cleaning oil

⓯ le masque hydratant mask

❶ **le réveil**   alarm clock

❷ **le cadre photo**   picture frame

❸ **la lampe**   lamp

❹ **la table de chevet**   nightstand

❺ **la tête de lit**   headboard

❻ **l'oreiller**   pillow

❼ **le lit pour deux personnes / le lit double**   double bed

❽ **le matelas**   mattress

❾ **le drap-housse**   sheet

❿ **le couette**   comforter, duvet

⓫ **les chaussons**   slippers

⓬ **la couverture en laine**   wool blanket

⓭ **le repose-pied**   footstool

⓮ **la commode**   chest of drawers

⓯ **le serre-livres**   bookend

⓰ **l'armoire à vêtement**   wardrobe

⓱ **les produits cosmétiques**   cosmetics

⓲ **la coiffeuse**   vanity

Additional Information: Kinds of Beds

1. **le lit pour une personne**
   single bed

2. **le canapé-lit**   sofa bed

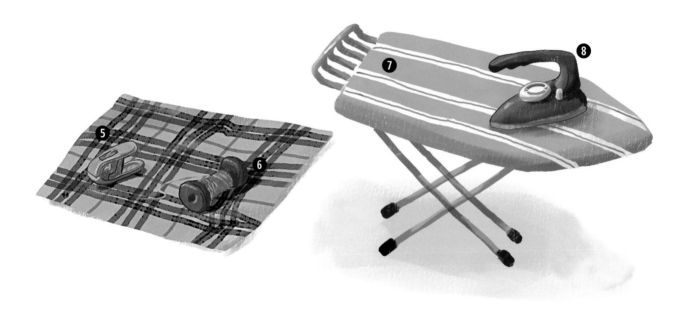

❶ **la lessive** laundry detergent

❷ **l'assouplissant** fabric softener

❸ **l'eau de javel** bleach

❹ **le cintre** hanger

❺ **la pince à linge** clothespin

❻ **le fil** thread

❼ **la planche à repasser** ironing board

❽ **le fer à repasser** iron

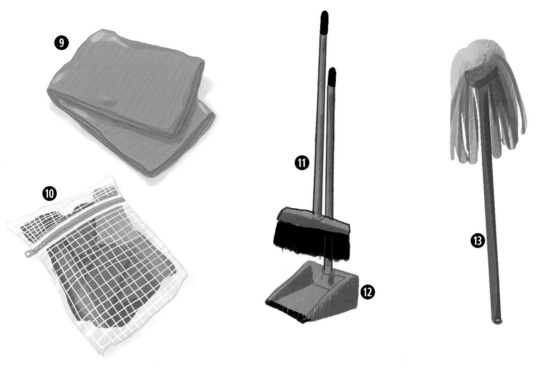

❾ le torchon rag

❿ le filet de lavage laundry bag

⓫ le balai broom

⓬ la pelle dustpan

⓭ le balai-serpillère mop

⓮ la machine à laver washing machine

⓯ le sèche-linge dryer

❶ **le réfrigérateur** refrigerator

❷ **le tablier** apron

❸ **la cafetière** coffeemaker

❹ **la hotte** range fan

❺ **le placard** cupboard

❻ **le four à micro-ondes** microwave oven

❼ **l'égouttoir** dishrack

❽ **la louche** ladle

❾ **le couperet** cleaver

❿ **la poêle** frying pan

⓫ **la gazinière** gas stove

⓬ **le wok** wok

⓭ **l'évier** sink

⓮ **le plan de travail** counter

⓯ **la planche à découper** cutting board

⓰ **le lave-vaisselle** dishwasher

⓱ **le four** oven

⓲ **la commode** cabinet

⓳ **la centrifugeuse** blender

⓴ **l'autocuiseur** steam cooker

㉑ **le thermos électrique**
electric thermos pot

㉒ **le grille-pain** toaster

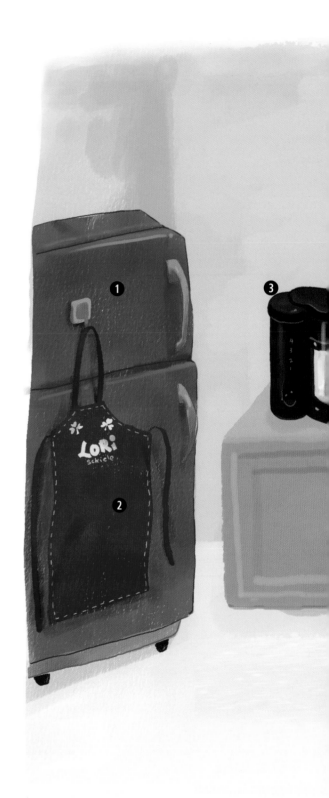

❶ le ruban adhésif tape

❷ le mètre ruban tape measure

❸ le crochet hook

❹ le tube fluorescent fluorescent light

❺ la hache ax

❻ le marteau hammer

❼ la perceuse electric drill

❽ la clef wrench

❾ la pince pliers

❿ le clou nail

⓫ la vis screw

⓬ le tournevis screwdriver

⓭ **la lampe de poche** flashlight

⓮ **la boîte à outils** toolbox

⓯ **la peinture** paint

⓰ **le pinceau** paintbrush

⓱ **le rouleau à peinture** paint roller

⓲ **l'échelle** ladder

⓳ **la pelle** shovel

⓴ **la brosse** scrub brush

㉑ **le seau** bucket

㉒ **l'éponge** sponge

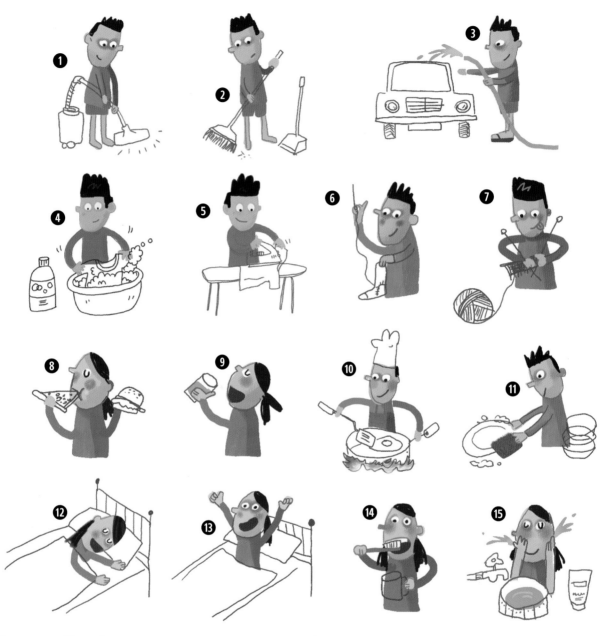

❶ **passer l'aspirateur** to vacuum

❷ **balayer** to sweep the floor

❸ **laver** to wash

❹ **laver le linge** to do the laundry

❺ **repasser le linge** to iron the clothes

❻ **coudre** to sew

❼ **tricoter** to knit

❽ **manger** to eat

❾ **boire** to drink

❿ **faire la cuisine** to cook

⓫ **faire la vaisselle** to wash the dishes

⓬ **se coucher** to sleep

⑬ se lever   to get up

⑭ se brosser les dents   to brush one's teeth

⑮ se laver le visage   to wash one's face

⑯ se doucher   to take a shower

⑰ s'habiller   to get dressed

⑱ porter   to wear (accessories)

⑲ se déshabiller   to take off

⑳ téléphoner   to call, to telephone

㉑ arroser   to water the plants

㉒ vider la poubelle   to take out the garbage

㉓ ouvrir / allumer   to open/ turn on

㉔ fermer / éteindre   to close/ turn off

❶ l'homme man

❷ la femme woman

❸ un homme âgé elderly man

❹ une femme âgée elderly woman

❺ une personne d'âge moyen
middle-aged person

❻ le garçon boy

❼ la fille girl

❽ l'adolescent teenager

❾ la femme enceinte pregnant woman

❿ le nourrisson toddler

⓫ l'enfant child

⓬ le bébé baby

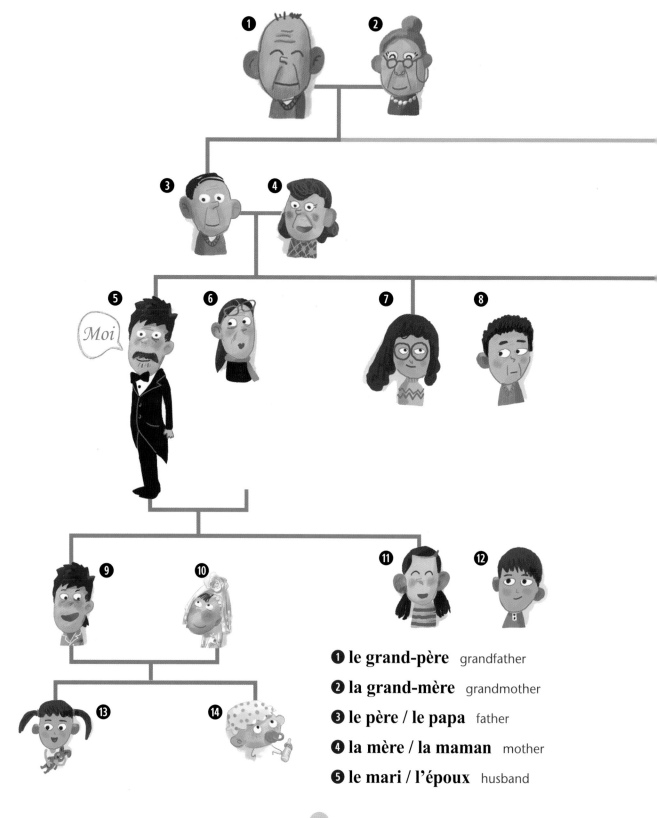

❶ le grand-père grandfather

❷ la grand-mère grandmother

❸ le père / le papa father

❹ la mère / la maman mother

❺ le mari / l'époux husband

les parents relatives

les parents parents

le conjoint / la conjointe spouse

les enfants children

le beau-père father-in-law

le beau-fils stepson

la belle-mère mother-in-law

la belle-fille stepdaughter

⓬ **le gendre** son-in-law

⓭ **la petite-fille** granddaughter

⓮ **le petit-fils** grandson

⓯ **la tante** aunt

⓰ **l'oncle** uncle

⓱ **le frère** brother

⓲ **la belle-sœur** sister-in-law

⓳ **le cousin** cousin (son of aunt and uncle)

⓴ **la cousine** cousin (daughter of aunt and uncle)

㉑ **le neveu** nephew

㉒ **la nièce** niece

❻ **la femme / l'épouse** wife

❼ **la sœur** sister

❽ **le beau-frère** brother-in-law

❾ **le fils** son

❿ **la belle-fille** daughter-in-law

⓫ **la fille** daughter

❶ le vendeur / la vendeuse
salesman, saleswoman

❷ l'assistant / l'assistante assistant

❸ le/la secrétaire secretary

❹ le/la gestionnaire manager

❺ le/la journaliste reporter

❻ le/la professeur teacher

❼ le / la professeur d'université
professor

❽ le/la fonctionnaire civil servant

❾ le policier police officer

❿ le pompier / le sapeur-pompier
firefighter

⓫ le/la militaire soldier

⑫ **le chauffeur / le routier / la chauffeuse / la routière** driver

⑬ **le/la pilote d'avion** pilot

⑭ **l'agriculteur / l'agricultrice** farmer

⑮ **le pêcheur / la pêcheuse** fisherman, fisherwoman

⑯ **le cuisinier / la cuisinière** chef

⑰ **l'architecte** architect

⑱ **le mécanicien / la mécanicienne** mechanic

⑲ **le menuisier / la menuisière** carpenter

⑳ **l'ouvrier / l'ouvrière** laborer

㉑ **le plombier / la plombière** plumber

❶ **le médecin** doctor

❷ **l'infirmier / l'infirmière** nurse

❸ **le/la scientifique** scientist

❹ **l'ingénieur / l'ingénieure** engineer

❺ **le politicien / la politicienne**
politician

❻ **l'homme d'affaires / la femme
d'affaires** businessman, businesswoman

❼ **l'entrepreneur / l'entrepreneuse**
entrepreneur

❽ **l'avocat / l'avocate** lawyer

❾ **le/la juge** judge

❿ **le/la guide** tour guide

⓫ **l'agent** broker, agent

⓬ **l'acteur / le comédien** actor

⓭ **l'actrice / la comédienne** actress

⓮ **le chanteur / la chanteuse** singer

⓯ **le coiffeur / la coiffeuse** hairstylist

⓰ **l'artiste** artist

⓱ **le musicien / la musicienne** musician

⓲ **le danseur / la danseuse** dancer

⓳ **le sculpteur / la sculptrice** sculptor

⓴ **le sportif / la sportive** athlete

THE INTERN

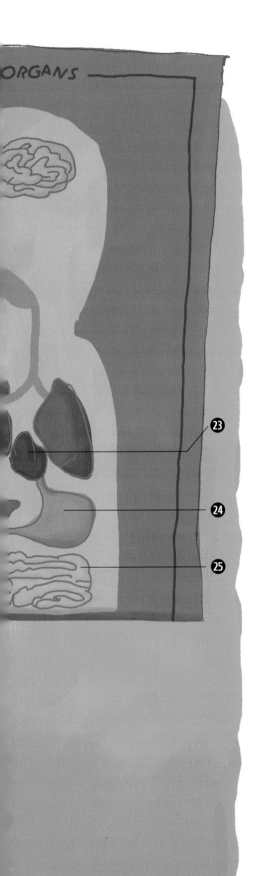

ORGANS

❶ **la tête** head

❷ **le cil** eyelash

❸ **l'œil (s.) / les yeux (p.)** eye

❹ **la joue** cheek

❺ **le cou** neck

❻ **la taille** waist

❼ **la main** hand

❽ **le pied** foot

❾ **les cheveux** hair

❿ **le front** forehead

⓫ **le sourcil** eyebrow

⓬ **le nez** nose

⓭ **la dent** tooth

⓮ **la bouche** mouth

⓯ **le menton** chin

⓰ **la poitrine** chest

⓱ **le ventre** belly

⓲ **le nombril** navel

⓳ **la cuisse** thigh

⓴ **le cerveau** brain

㉑ **le poumon** lung

㉒ **le foie** liver

㉓ **le cœur** heart

㉔ **l'estomac** stomach

㉕ **l'intestin** intestines

❶ **content** happy

❷ **excité** excited

❸ **détendu** relaxed

❹ **surpris** surprised

❺ **en colère** angry

❻ **embarrassé** embarrassed

7

8

9

10

11

12

7 timide shy

8 nerveux nervous

9 sourire to smile

10 rire to laugh

11 pleurer to cry

12 triste sad

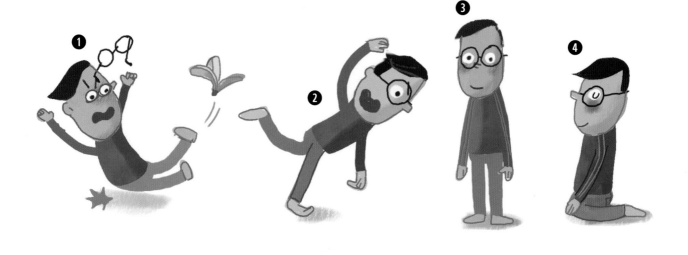

❶ glisser to slip

❷ tomber to fall down

❸ être debout to stand

❹ se mettre à genoux to kneel

❺ s'accroupir to squat

❻ se mettre sur les mains
to do a handstand

❼ marcher to walk

❽ ramper to crawl

❾ sauter to jump

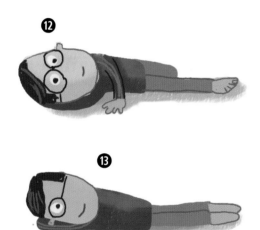

❿ **taper avec le pied** to kick

⓫ **être assis** to sit

⓬ **s'allonger** to lie down

⓭ **se mettre à plat ventre** to lie facedown

⓮ **porter sur son dos**
to carry (something) on (one's) back

⓯ **s'étirer** to stretch

❶ **la porte tourniquet** turnstile

❷ **les produits surgelés** frozen foods

❸ **les produits laitiers** dairy products

❹ **les boissons** beverages

❺ **les produits en conserves** canned food

❻ **les aliments emballés** packaged food

❼ **le pain** bread

❽ **les plats à réchauffer** microwave food

❾ **le sac à provisions** shopping bag

❿ **la carte de fidélité** membership card

⓫ **les échantillons alimentaires**
free sample

⓬ **la viande** meat

⓭ **les fruits de mer** seafood

⓮ **les légumes** vegetables

⓯ **les fruits** fruit

⓰ **le caddie** shopping cart

⓱ **le client** customer

⓲ **le panier** basket

⓳ **la caisse enregistreuse** cash register

⓴ **le lecteur de code-barres** scanner

㉑ **le caissier / la caissière** cashier

㉒ **le sac en plastique** plastic bag

㉓ **le liquide** cash

㉔ **le reçu** receipt

㉕ **les plats chauds** deli food

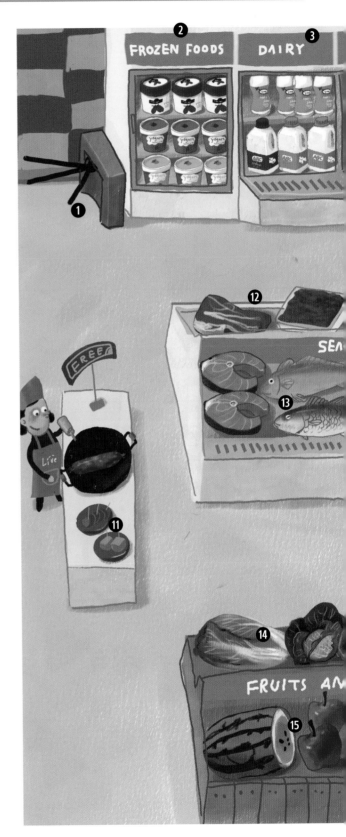

❶ l'ananas pineapple

❷ la prune plum

❸ la fraise strawberry

❹ la cerise cherry

❺ le melon melon

❻ le cantaloup cantaloupe

❼ la pastèque watermelon

❽ la papaye papaya

❾ la mangue mango

❿ le kaki persimmon

⓫ la poire pear

⓬ le kiwi kiwi fruit

⓭ le citron lemon

⓮ le fruit de la passion passion fruit

❶❺ **la mandarine** tangerine

❶❻ **l'orange** orange

❶❼ **le pamplemousse** grapefruit

❶❽ **le raisin** grapes

❶❾ **la carambole** star fruit

❷⓿ **la pomme** apple

❷❶ **la banane** banana

❷❷ **la goyave** guava

❷❸ **la myrtille** blueberries

❷❹ **la framboise** raspberry

❷❺ **la pêche** peach

❷❻ **l'abricot** apricot

❷❼ **la grenade** pomegranate

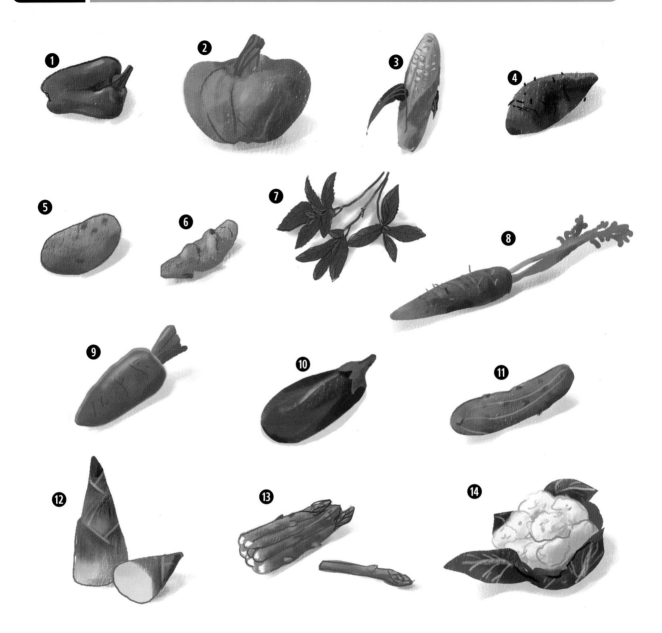

❶ le poivron green pepper

❷ la citrouille pumpkin

❸ le maïs corn

❹ la patate douce sweet potato

❺ la pomme de terre potato

❻ le gingembre ginger

❼ le basilic basil

❽ la carotte carrot

❾ le radis radish

❿ l'aubergine eggplant

⓫ le concombre cucumber

⓬ les pousses de bambou bamboo shoot

⓭ l'asperge asparagus

⓮ le chou-fleur cauliflower

⑮ le chou   cabbage

⑯ la laitue   lettuce

⑰ les germes de soja   bean sprouts

⑱ le brocoli   broccoli

⑲ les épinards   spinach

⑳ le champignon   mushroom

㉑ la tomate   tomato

㉒ le céleri   celery

㉓ l'oignon   onion

㉔ la ciboule   green onion

㉕ l'ail   garlic

㉖ les choux de Bruxelles   brussels sprouts

㉗ le chou rouge   red cabbage

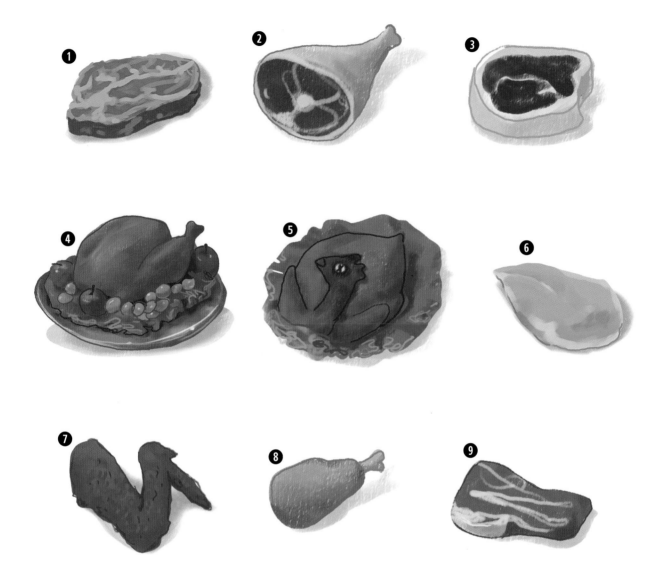

❶ l'agneau lamb

❷ le gigot leg of lamb

❸ le bœuf beef

❹ la dinde turkey

❺ le poulet chicken

❻ le blanc de poulet chicken breast

❼ l'aile de poulet chicken wing

❽ la cuisse de poulet chicken leg

❾ le porc pork

⑩ **la viande hachée** ground meat

⑪ **la côtelette** ribs

⑫ **la boulette de viande** meatballs

⑬ **le bacon** bacon

⑭ **le jambon** ham

⑮ **le hot dog** hot dog

⑯ **la saucisse** sausage

⑰ **le salami** salami

⑱ **la viande séchée** jerky

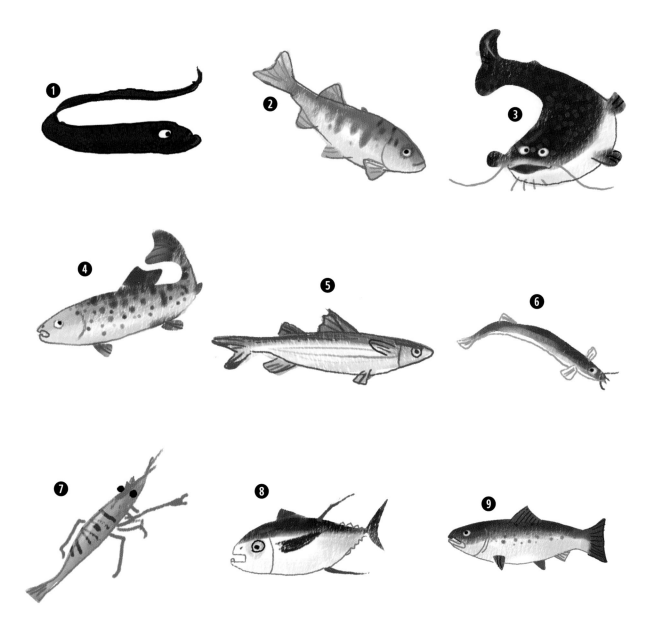

❶ **l'anguille** eel

❷ **la truite** trout

❸ **le silure** catfish

❹ **le mérou** grouper

❺ **le mulet** gray mullet

❻ **la loche** loach

❼ **la crevette** shrimp

❽ **le thon** tuna

❾ **le saumon** salmon

⑩ la morue cod

⑪ l'ormeau abalone

⑫ la coquille Saint-Jacques scallop

⑬ l'huître oyster

⑭ la palourde clam

⑮ la boulette de poisson fish ball

⑯ la sole (Dover) sole

⑰ le calmar / le calamar squid

⑱ le poulpe octopus

❶ le cola cola

❷ le soda soda

❸ le smoothie smoothie

❹ le café coffee

❺ le chocolat chaud hot chocolate

❻ le thé glacé iced tea

❼ l'eau minérale mineral water

❽ la citronnade lemonade

❾ le jus de fruit juice

❶ **le beurre** butter

❷ **la crème** cream

❸ **la glace** ice cream

❹ **le bâtonnet glacé** frozen treat

❺ **le fromage** cheese

❻ **le yaourt** yogurt

❼ **le yaourt à boire** drinking yogurt

❽ **le milk-shake** milk shake

❾ **le lait écrémé** non-fat milk, skim milk

❿ **le lait demi-écrémé** low-fat milk

⓫ **le lait entier** whole milk

❶ les cornichons pickles

❷ les serviettes en papier paper napkins

❸ la paille straw

❹ le sac de vente à emporter
doggie bag

❺ les pancakes pancakes

❻ les nuggets de poulet chicken nuggets

❼ les beignets doughnuts

❽ les rondelles d'oignon frites onion rings

❾ le croissant croissant

❿ à emporter to go

⓫ le tabouret stool

⑫ **le hamburger** hamburger

⑬ **sur place** for here

⑭ **les frites** french fries

⑮ **le plateau** serving tray

⑯ **le bagel** bagel

⑰ **le poulet frit** fried chicken

⑱ **les muffins** muffins

⑲ **la gaufre** waffle

53

❶ le serveur waiter

❷ le glaçon ice cube

❸ le seau à glace ice bucket

❹ la théière teapot

❺ la cafetière coffeepot

❻ la serveuse waitress

❼ la nappe tablecloth

❽ la carte menu

❾ **le poivrier**   pepper shaker

❿ **la salière**   salt shaker

⓫ **l'addition**   bill

⓬ **les cure-dents**   toothpicks

⓭ **le set de table**   place mat

⓮ **la serviette de table**   napkin

⓯ **le maître d'hôtel**   hostess

⓰ **le comptoir**   counter

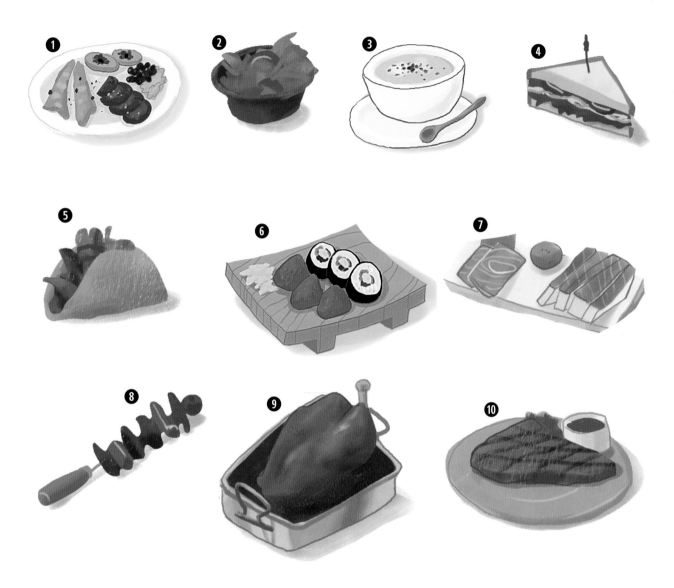

❶ le hors d'œuvre appetizer

❷ la salade salad

❸ la soupe soup

❹ le sandwich sandwich

❺ le taco taco

❻ le sushi sushi

❼ le sashimi sashimi

❽ la brochette shish kebab

❾ le poulet rôti roast chicken

❿ le steak steak

⓫ les lasagnes lasagna

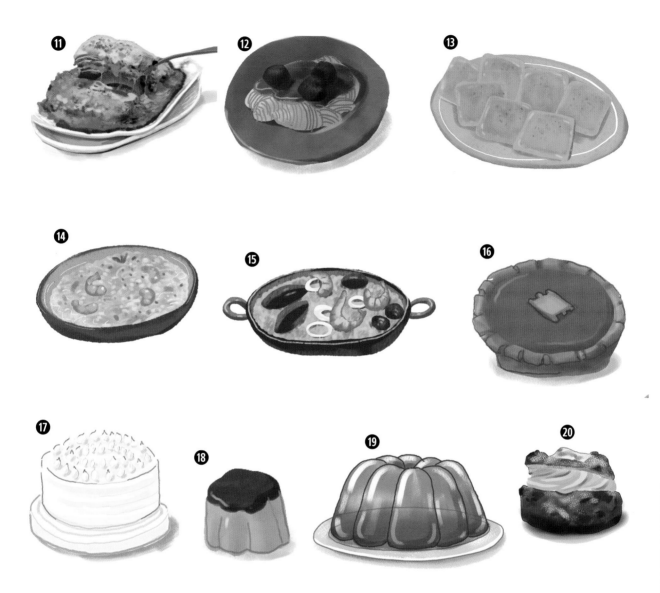

⑫ **les spaghettis** spaghetti

⑬ **les raviolis** ravioli

⑭ **le risotto** risotto

⑮ **la paella** paella

⑯ **la tarte aux pommes** apple pie

⑰ **le gâteau** cake

⑱ **le flan** pudding

⑲ **la gélatine** gelatin

⑳ **le chou à la crème** cream puff

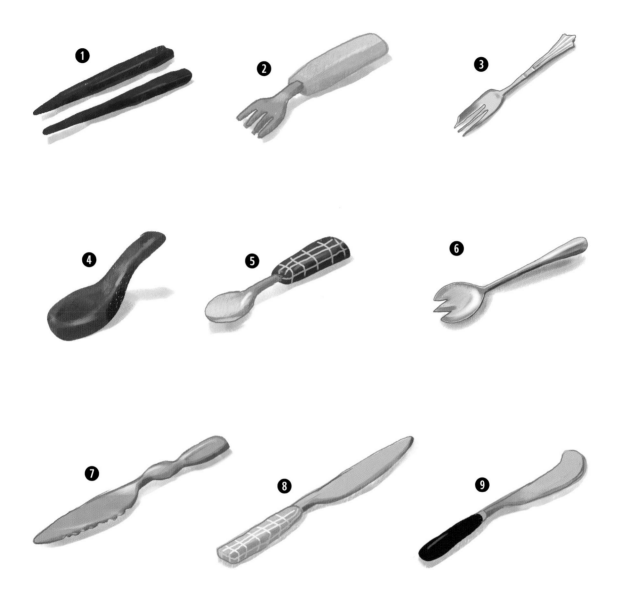

❶ **les baguettes** chopsticks

❷ **la fourchette** fork

❸ **la fourchette à dessert** dessert fork

❹ **la cuillère à soupe** spoon

❺ **la cuillère à café** teaspoon

❻ **la cuillère à salade** salad spoon

❼ **le couteau à viande** steak knife

❽ **le couteau de table** dinner knife

❾ **le couteau à beurre** butter knife

❿ **le bol** bowl

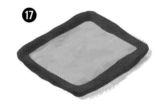

⑩ **le plateau** platter

⑫ **l'assiette** plate

⑬ **l'assiette creuse** soup plate

⑭ **la soucoupe** saucer

⑮ **le verre** water glass

⑯ **le mug** mug

⑰ **le sous-verre** beverage coaster

❶ **cuire au four**   to bake

❷ **rôtir**   to grill

❸ **cuire au barbecue**   to barbecue

❹ **frire**   to fry

❺ **sauter**   to stir-fry

❻ **poêler**   to pan-fry

❼ **mijoter**   to simmer

❽ **bouillir**   to boil

❾ **blanchir**   to blanch

❿ **cuire à petit feu / cuire à feu doux**
to stew

⓫ **cuire à la vapeur**   to steam

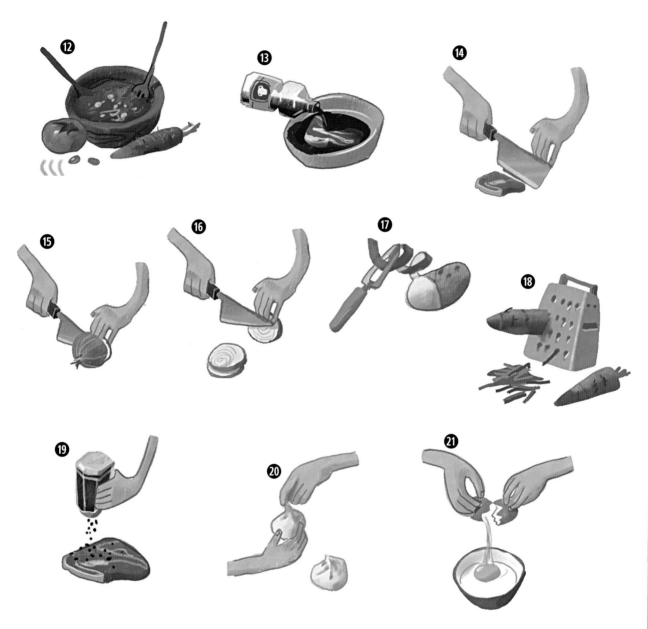

⑫ **mélanger** to toss

⑬ **mariner** to marinate

⑭ **hacher** to chop

⑮ **couper** to cut

⑯ **trancher** to slice

⑰ **éplucher** to peel

⑱ **râper** to grate

⑲ **saupoudrer** to sprinkle

⑳ **envelopper** to wrap

㉑ **casser les œufs** to crack (an egg)

❶ le cristal de sucre rock sugar

❷ la cassonade brown sugar

❸ le sel salt

❹ le poivre pepper

❺ le vinaigre vinegar

❻ le vin wine

❼ l'huile de cuisson cooking oil

❽ l'huile d'olive olive oil

❾ la sauce soja soy sauce

❿ l'huile de sésame sesame oil

⓫ la sauce nuoc mam fish sauce

  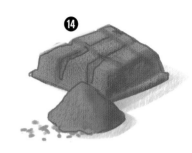

⑫ la farine de maïs cornstarch

⑬ la fécule de pomme de terre
potato starch

⑭ le curry curry

⑮ la moutarde mustard

⑯ le ketchup ketchup

⑰ le wasabi wasabi

⑱ la sauce pimentée chili sauce

⑲ la cannelle cinnamon

⑳ le caviar caviar

❶ la robe dress

❷ la robe de cérémonie gown

❸ le costume occidental suit

❹ la chemise shirt

❺ le gilet vest

❻ le T-shirt T-shirt

❼ la jupe skirt

❽ le pantalon pants

❾ le jean jeans

❿ le short shorts

⑪ le caleçon boxers

⑫ le pull sweater

⑬ la veste jacket

⑭ la doudoune down coat

⑮ le survêtement sportswear

⑯ l'uniforme uniform

⑰ l'imperméable raincoat

⑱ le pyjama pajamas

⑲ le soutien-gorge bra

⑳ la culotte underwear

❶ **le chapeau** hat

❷ **le bandeau** bandana

❸ **l'élastique à cheveux** hair band

❹ **l'épingle à cheveux** hair clip

❺ **la boucle d'oreille** earrings

❻ **le voile** veil

❼ **les lunettes** eyeglasses

❽ **les lunettes de soleil** sunglasses

❾ **le sac à main** purse

❿ **le portefeuille** wallet

⓫ **le sac à dos** backpack

⓬ **l'écharpe** scarf

⓭ **le foulard** silk scarf

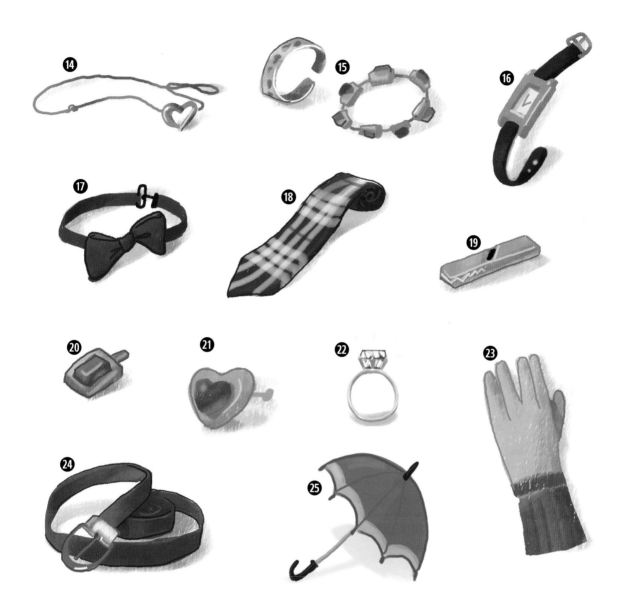

⓮ **le collier** necklace

⓯ **la gourmette / le bracelet** bracelet

⓰ **la montre** wristwatch

⓱ **le nœud papillon** bow tie

⓲ **la cravate** necktie

⓳ **l'épingle de cravate** tie clip

⓴ **le bouton de manchette** cuff link

㉑ **la broche** brooch

㉒ **la bague** ring

㉓ **le gant** glove

㉔ **la ceinture** belt

㉕ **le parapluie** umbrella

❶ **les chaussures** shoes

❷ **les chaussures en cuir** leather shoes

❸ **les chaussures à talon** high heels

❹ **les souliers à bout pointu**
   pointed shoes

❺ **les converse** canvas shoes

❻ **les bottines** boots

❼ **les chaussures de sport / les baskets**
   sneakers

❽ **les sandales** sandals

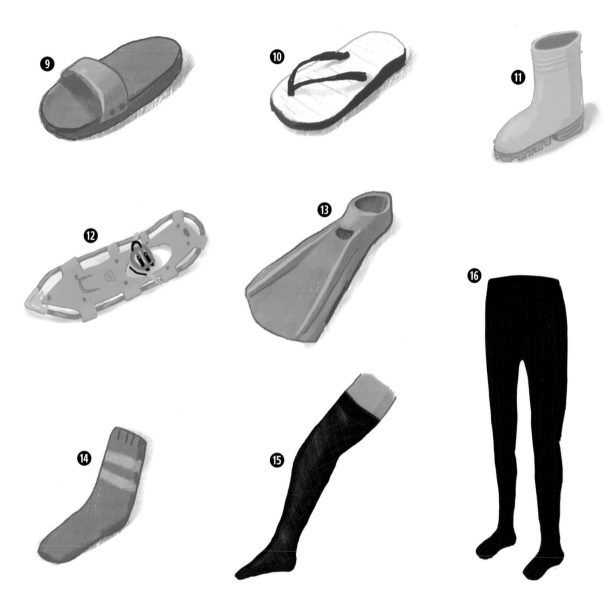

❾ **les pantoufles** slippers

❿ **les tongs** flip-flops

⓫ **les bottes de pluie** rain boots

⓬ **les raquettes** snowshoes

⓭ **les palmes** flippers

⓮ **les chaussettes** socks

⓯ **les bas** stockings

⓰ **les collants** panty hose

❶ **le centre commercial** department store

❷ **le karaoké** karaoke bar

❸ **la rue** street

❹ **le magasin d'électroménager** appliance store

❺ **la supérette** convenience store

❻ **le restaurant** restaurant

❼ **la banque** bank

❽ **l'hôpital** hospital

❾ **la poste** post office

❿ **le distributeur automatique** vending machine

⓫ **l'hôtel** hotel

⓬ **la salle de gymnastique** gym

⑬ la librairie bookstore

⑭ le magasin de meubles furniture store

⑮ la boîte de nuit nightclub

⑯ le salon de thé tea house

⑰ le café coffee shop

⑱ la pharmacie pharmacy

⑲ le cinéma movie theater

⑳ le poste de police police station

㉑ le magasin de jouets toy store

㉒ la boulangerie bakery

㉓ le salon de coiffure beauty salon

㉔ l'épicerie fine delicatessen

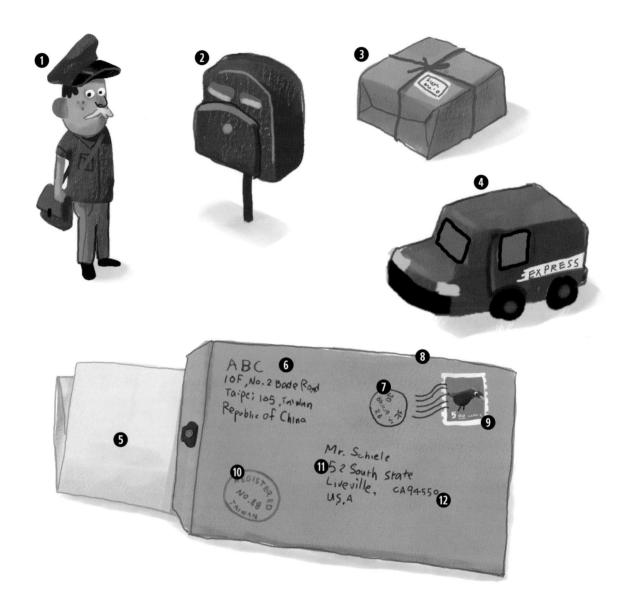

1 **le facteur** letter carrier

2 **la boîte aux lettres** mailbox

3 **le colis** package

4 **le courrier express** express mail

5 **la lettre** letter

6 **l'adresse de l'expéditeur**
return address

7 **le cachet de la poste** postmark

8 **l'enveloppe** envelope

9 **le timbre** stamp

10 **la lettre en recommandé** registered mail

11 **l'adresse du destinataire**
recipient's address

12 **le code postal** zip code

⑬ **le courrier aérien** airmail letter

⑭ **la lettre ordinaire** ordinary mail

⑮ **la carte postale** postcard

⑯ **la carte** card

⑰ **par bateau** maritime mail

⑱ **par avion** airmail

⑲ **le mail / le courrier électronique**
e-mail

⑳ **le sms / le texto** text message

❶ **le poste de police**   police station

❷ **le policier en civil**   plainclothes officer

❸ **l'agent de circulation**   traffic officer

❹ **le képi**   police cap

❺ **le sifflet**   whistle

❻ **le brassard**   patch

❼ **le badge**   badge

❽ **le pistolet**   gun

❾ **la matraque**   police baton

❿ **les menottes**   handcuffs

⑪ **le voleur** thief

⑫ **la patrouille** patrol officer

⑬ **le chien policier** police dog

⑭ **le motard** police motorcycle

⑮ **la voiture de police** patrol car

⑯ **porter plainte** to call the police

⑰ **le bandit** robber

⑱ **faire une déposition** written report

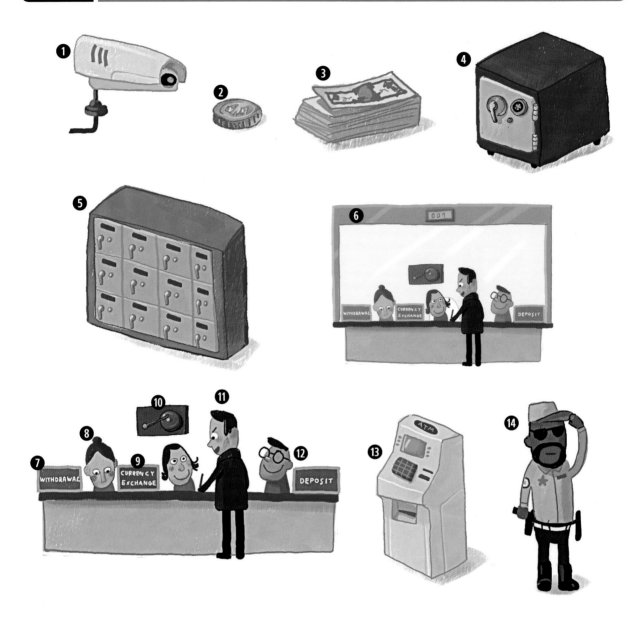

❶ la caméra de surveillance
security camera

❷ la pièce coin

❸ le billet bill

❹ le coffre safe

❺ le coffre-fort safe-deposit box

❻ la fenêtre du guichet counter, window

❼ le retrait withdrawal

❽ le caissier / la caissière teller

❾ l'échange de devises currency exchange

❿ l'alarme alarm

⓫ ouvrir un compte to open an account

⓬ le dépôt deposit

⓭ le distributeur automatique ATM

 ⑮

 ⑯

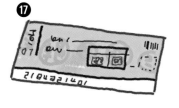 ⑰

 ⑱

 ⑲

 ⑳

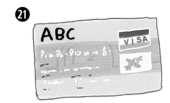 ㉑

 ㉒

 ㉓

 ㉔

㉕

USD	🇺🇸	33.400	33.940	34.440
JPY	●	28.440	28.740	29.340
EUR	🇪🇺	45.520	45.770	46.620
TWD	✹	0.840	—	1.150

⑭ **l'agent de sécurité** security guard

⑮ **la voiture blindée** armored truck

⑯ **le mandat** money order

⑰ **le chèque** check

⑱ **le chèque-voyage** traveler's check

⑲ **le livret bancaire** passbook

⑳ **la carte de retrait** ATM card

㉑ **la carte de paiement** credit card

㉒ **la pièce d'identité** ID card

㉓ **le tampon** stamp

㉔ **la signature** signature

㉕ **le taux de change** exchange rate

❶ l'ascenseur elevator

❷ la vitrine display counter

❸ l'employé salesclerk

❹ les vêtements pour femme
women's department

❺ les sous-vêtements lingerie department

❻ le bureau des objets trouvés
lost-and-found department

❼ l'escalator escalator

❽ l'électroménager
household appliances department

❾ le mobilier furnishing department

❿ les vêtements pour adolescent
teen department

⓫ les articles de sport
sporting-goods department

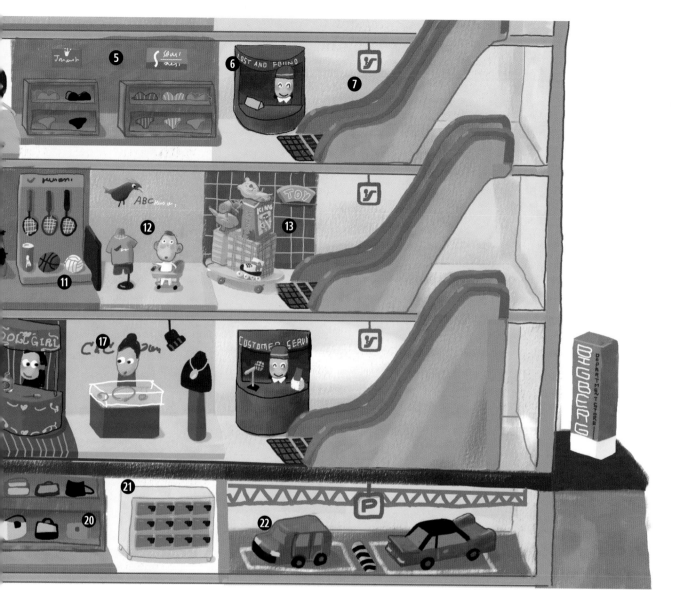

⑫ **les vêtements pour enfant**
children's department

⑬ **les jouets**   toy department

⑭ **les vêtements pour homme**
men's department

⑮ **le point accueil / le point
informations**   information desk

⑯ **les cosmétiques**   cosmetics department

⑰ **les bijoux**   jewelry department

⑱ **les chaussures**   shoe department

⑲ **l'alimentation**   food court

⑳ **les articles en cuir**
leather goods department

㉑ **la consigne / le casier**   lockers

㉒ **le parking souterrain**
underground parking garage

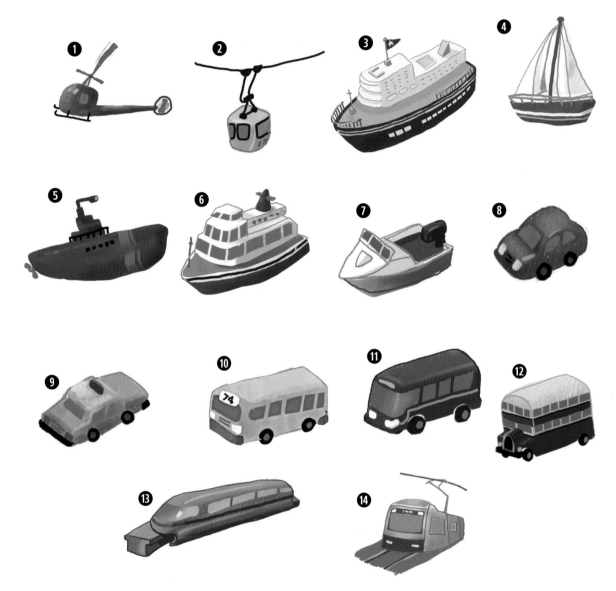

❶ l'hélicoptère helicopter

❷ le téléphérique cable car

❸ le bateau de croisière ocean liner

❹ le voilier sailboat

❺ le sous-marin submarine

❻ le ferry ferry

❼ le bateau à moteur motorboat

❽ la voiture car

❾ le taxi taxi

❿ le bus bus

⓫ le car tour bus

⓬ le car à deux étages double-decker bus

⓭ le monorail monorail

⓮ le tramway tram

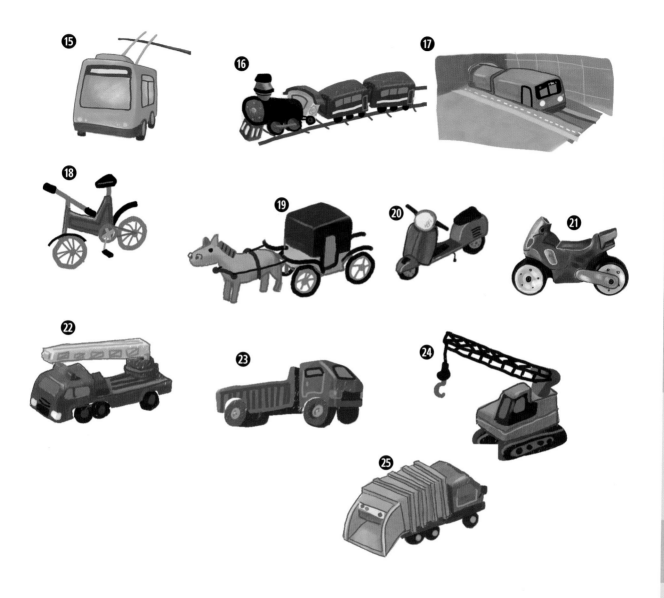

⑮ le trolley trolley bus

⑯ le train train

⑰ le métro subway

⑱ le vélo bicycle

⑲ la charrette / le carrosse
horse-drawn carriage

⑳ le scooter scooter

㉑ la moto motorcycle

㉒ le camion de pompiers fire engine

㉓ le camion truck

㉔ la grue crane

**㉕ le camion à ordures / le camion
poubelle** garbage truck

❶ le parc park

❷ la passerelle pedestrian bridge

❸ le coin (de la rue) corner

❹ le panneau de signalisation routière
street sign

❺ la bouche de métro subway entrance

❻ la route road

❼ le trottoir sidewalk

❽ l'arrêt de bus bus stop

❾ la station essence gas station

❿ l'autoroute freeway

⓫ la voiture de sport sports car

⓬ le carrefour intersection

⓭ le passage piéton crosswalk

⓮ le lampadaire streetlight

⓯ le feu tricolore traffic light

⓰ l'arcade arcade

⓱ le passage souterrain underpass

⓲ la bordure de route curb

⓳ la place (de parking) parking space

❶ les toilettes / les cabinets / les WC
lavatory, toilet

❷ le personnel navigant flight attendant

❸ la sortie de secours
emergency exit

❹ la visière window blind

❺ la tablette tray

❻ la pochette du siège seat pocket

❼ le gilet de sauvetage
life preserver

**❽ le casier à bagages / le compartiment
à bagages** overhead compartment

❾ la place côté hublot window seat

❿ la place côté couloir aisle seat

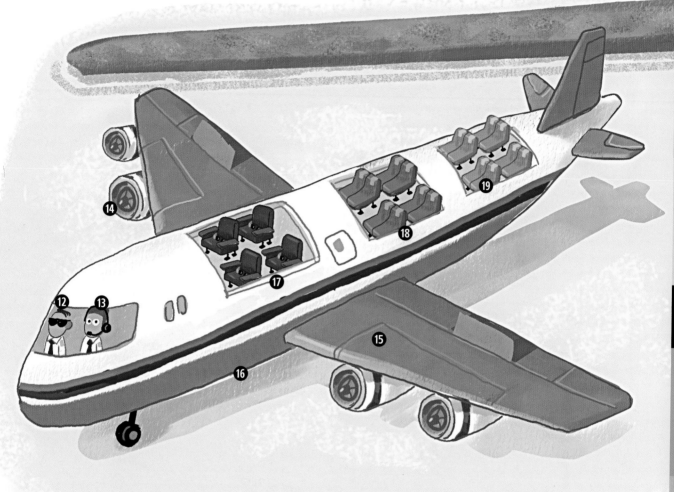

⑪ la ceinture de sécurité seat belt

⑫ le copilote copilot

⑬ le pilote captain

⑭ le réacteur jet engine

⑮ l'aile wing

⑯ le fuselage fuselage

⑰ la première classe first class

⑱ la classe business business class

⑲ la classe économique economy class

❶ le terminal terminal

❷ le bureau de change currency exchange

❸ le comptoir des assurances
insurance counter

❹ le comptoir d'enregistrement
check-in counter

❺ l'atterrissage landing

❻ l'avion airplane

❼ le comptoir de la compagnie aérienne
airline service counter

❽ le passager passenger

❾ l'agent (d'escale) airline representative

❿ la valise luggage

⓫ le chariot luggage cart

⓬ le bagagier skycap

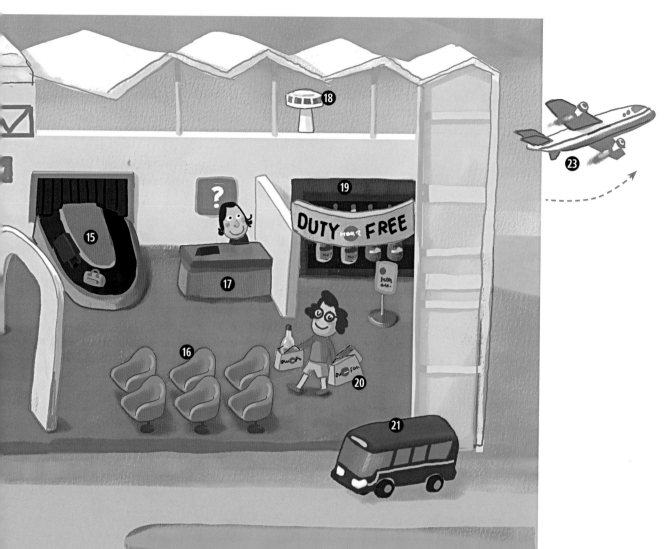

⑬ la douane customs

⑭ l'immigration immigration

⑮ le carrousel à bagages
luggage carousel

⑯ le hall des départs departure lobby

**⑰ le point accueil / le point
informations** information desk

⑱ la tour de contrôle control tower

⑲ le magasin hors taxe duty-free shop

⑳ le produit hors taxe duty-free item

㉑ le bus (de l'aéroport) shuttle bus

㉒ la piste d'atterrissage runway

㉓ le décollage takeoff

❶ jouer aux échecs to play chess

❷ jouer aux échecs chinois
to play Chinese checkers

❸ jouer aux cartes to play cards

❹ jouer au mah-jong to play mahjong

❺ peindre to paint

❻ sculpter to sculpt

❼ danser to dance

❽ faire de la randonnée (en montagne)
hiking

❾ faire de l'alpinisme mountain climbing

❿ faire du camping camping

⓫ pêcher to fish

⓬ faire du jardinage gardening

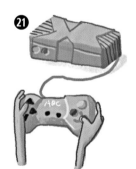

⑬ **observer les oiseaux** to bird-watch

⑭ **chanter** to sing

⑮ **faire du lèche-vitrines** window shopping

⑯ **faire de la photographie** to photograph

⑰ **lire** to read

⑱ **écouter de la musique** to listen to music

⑲ **regarder la télévision** to watch TV

⑳ **aller au cinéma / regarder un film** to watch movies (in the cinema) / to watch movies (at home)

㉑ **jouer aux jeux vidéo** to play video games

㉒ **surfer sur internet** to surf the Internet

❶ le saxophone saxophone

❷ la flûte traversière flute

❸ la clarinette clarinet

❹ le hautbois oboe

❺ le trombone trombone

❻ le cor d'harmonie French horn

❼ la trompette trumpet

❽ le tuba tuba

❾ l'harmonica harmonica

❿ la guitare guitar

⑪ la guitare basse   bass guitar

⑫ la harpe   harp

⑬ le violon   violin

⑭ le violoncelle   cello

⑮ le piano   piano

⑯ le synthétiseur   electric keyboard

⑰ l'accordéon   accordion

⑱ le tambourin   tambourine

⑲ le tambour   drum

⑳ le xylophone   xylophone

❶ l'ambulance ambulance

❷ la chambre d'hôpital ward

❸ le patient patient

❹ l'ORL ear, nose, and throat doctor

❺ la salle d'opération operating room

❻ l'unité de soins intensifs ICU

❼ le dentiste dentist

❽ le pédiatre pediatrician

❾ l'obstétricien obstetrician

❿ l'ophtalmologue ophthalmologist

⓫ le médecin interne
internal medicine specialist

⓬ le chirurgien surgeon

⑬ **l'infirmerie**   nurses' station

⑭ **l'infirmier / l'infirmière**   nurse

⑮ **les béquilles**   crutch

⑯ **le déambulateur**   walker

⑰ **le fauteuil roulant**   wheelchair

⑱ **le guichet d'inscription**   reception

⑲ **le dossier médical**
patient information form

⑳ **la salle d'attente**   waiting room

㉑ **le brancard**   stretcher

㉒ **la salle d'urgences**   emergency room

❶ l'école primaire elementary school

❷ le directeur de l'école principal

❸ sortir de l'école to get out from school

❹ l'école maternelle kindergarten

❺ aller à l'école to attend school

❻ la cour de récréation playground

❼ le lycée senior high school

❽ la fin du cours to get out from class

❾ l'école publique public school

❿ l'école privée private school

⓫ le collège junior high school

⓬ le transfert de scolarité to transfer to another school

⑬ l'ancien élève alumnus

⑭ l'institut graduate school

⑮ la division de la formation continue
institute of continuing education

⑯ la licence bachelor's degree

⑰ le master master's degree

⑱ le doctorat doctorate

⑲ le doyen dean

⑳ le directeur du département
department chair

㉑ le chercheur scholar

㉒ l'université / la faculté / la fac university

㉓ la classe des langues language class

㉔ être en cours to have class

❶ le stade field

❷ la piste d'athlétisme track

❸ le terrain de basket basketball court

❹ la statue statue

❺ la porte de l'école school gate

❻ le tableau d'affichage bulletin board

❼ le bureau office

❽ le bureau du directeur principal's office

❾ la salle de classe classroom

❿ la maison des langues language lab

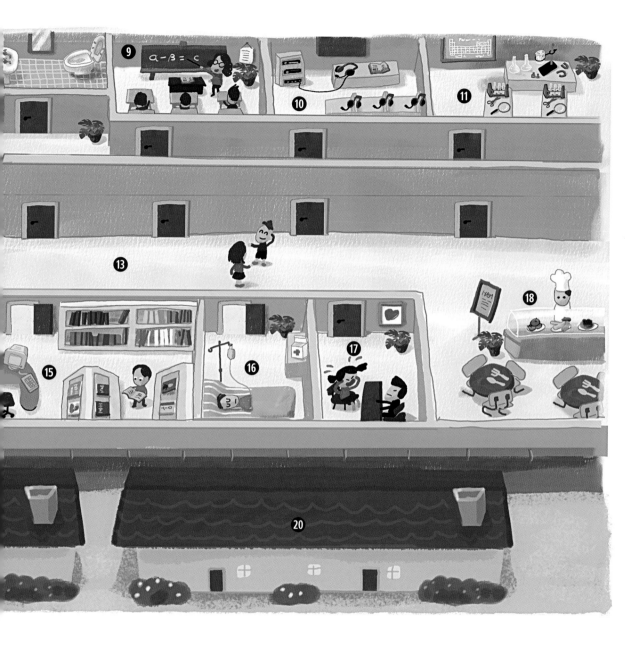

⑪ le laboratoire (de chimie) (chemistry) lab

⑫ les casiers lockers

⑬ le couloir hallway

⑭ l'auditorium auditorium

⑮ la bibliothèque library

⑯ l'infirmerie nurse's office

⑰ le bureau du conseiller d'orientation guidance counselor's office

⑱ la cafétéria cafeteria

⑲ le gymnase gymnasium

⑳ le dortoir dormitory

Part I Courses · Les cours

❶ la matière subject

❷ le français French

❸ le chinois Chinese

❹ l'anglais English

❺ le japonais Japanese

❻ l'espagnol Spanish

❼ la langue étrangère
foreign language

❽ la linguistique linguistics

❾ la philosophie philosophy

❿ la littérature literature

⓫ les mathématiques math

⓬ l'économie economics

⓭ l'ingénierie engineering

⓮ l'architecture architecture

⓯ la géographie geography

⓰ l'histoire history

⓱ l'astronomie astronomy

⓲ la physique physics

⓳ la chimie chemistry

⓴ la biologie biology

㉑ la médecine medicine

㉒ le droit law

㉓ les sciences politiques political science

㉔ la sociologie sociology

㉕ la musique music

㉖ le sport physical education

Part II Campus Life · La vie dans le campus

❶ **l'année scolaire** semester

❷ **le devoir** homework

❸ **la composition** essay

❹ **l'examen** exam

❺ **le contrôle continu** monthly test

❻ **l'examen de mi-semestre**
midterm

❼ **l'examen de fin semestre**
final exam

❽ **l'exposé** oral presentation

❾ **le groupe de discussion**
group discussion

❿ **la dictée** dictation

⓫ **tricher** to cheat

⓬ **réussir** to pass

⓭ **échouer** to fail

⓮ **la bourse** scholarship

⓯ **les activités extra-scolaires**
extracurricular activities

⓰ **avoir un petit boulot / un job
étudiant** part-time job

⓱ **délivrer un diplômé** to graduate

1. **le tableau noir** chalkboard
2. **la craie** chalk
3. **l'éponge** eraser
4. **l'estrade** platform
5. **la gomme** (pencil) eraser
6. **le sous-main** desk mat
7. **la boîte à crayons** pencil case
8. **le micro(phone)** microphone
9. **le livre** book
10. **le rétroprojecteur** projector
11. **le manuel** textbook
12. **la chaise** chair
13. **le globe** globe
14. **la carte** map
15. **l'étagère** book rack

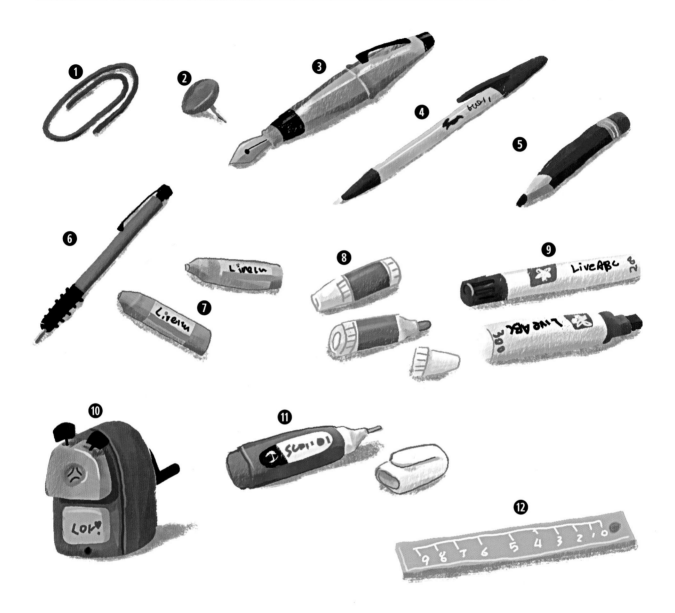

❶ **le trombone** paper clip

❷ **la punaise** thumbtack

❸ **le stylo plume** fountain pen

❹ **le stylo bille** ballpoint pen

❺ **le crayon à papier** pencil

❻ **le portemine** mechanical pencil

❼ **la craie grasse** crayon

❽ **le stylo de couleur** color pen

❾ **le marqueur** marker

❿ **le taille-crayon** pencil sharpener

⓫ **le correcteur liquide** correction fluid

⓬ **la règle** ruler

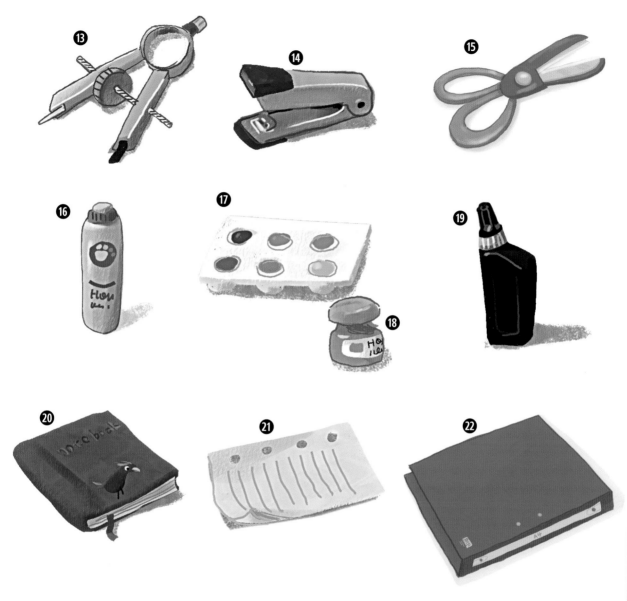

13 **le compas** compass

14 **l'agrafeuse** stapler

15 **les ciseaux** scissors

16 **la colle** glue

17 **la palette de couleurs** paint palette

18 **le pigment** paint

19 **l'encre** ink

20 **le bloc-notes** notebook

21 **le feuillet mobile** sheet of paper

22 **le classeur** folder

❶ **rouge** red

❷ **rose** pink

❸ **orange** orange

❹ **jaune** yellow

❺ **vert** green

❻ **bleu** blue

❼ **violet** purple

❽ **marron** brown

❾ **noir** black

❿ **blanc** white

⓫ **gris** gray

⓬ **beige** beige

⓭ **argenté** silver

⓮ **doré** gold

⓯ **foncé** dark

⓰ **clair** light

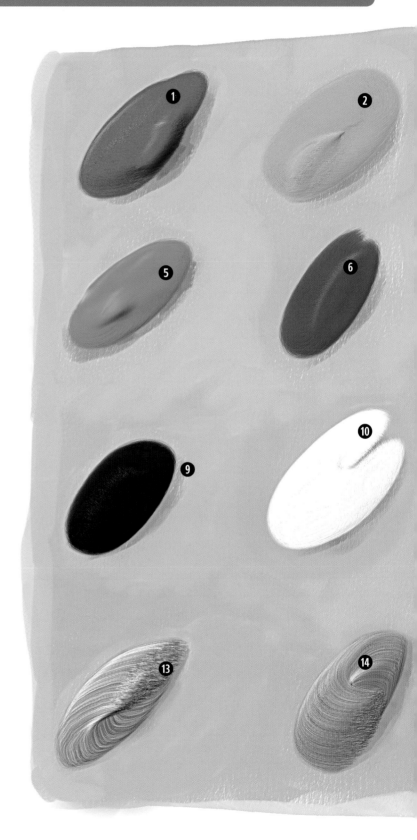

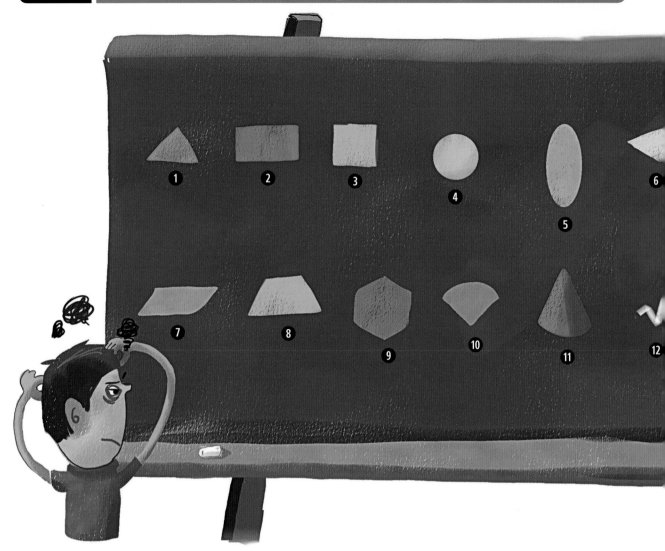

1. **le triangle** triangle
2. **le rectangle** rectangle
3. **le carré** square
4. **le cercle** circle
5. **l'ovale** oval
6. **le losange** diamond
7. **le parallélogramme** parallelogram
8. **le trapèze** trapezoid
9. **le polygone** polygon
10. **le secteur circulaire** sector

11. **le cône** cone
12. **la racine carrée** square root symbol
13. **plus** plus
14. **moins** minus
15. **multiplier** multiplication
16. **diviser** division
17. **supérieur à** greater than
18. **inférieur à** less than
19. **égal** equal
20. **le point d'exclamation** exclamation point

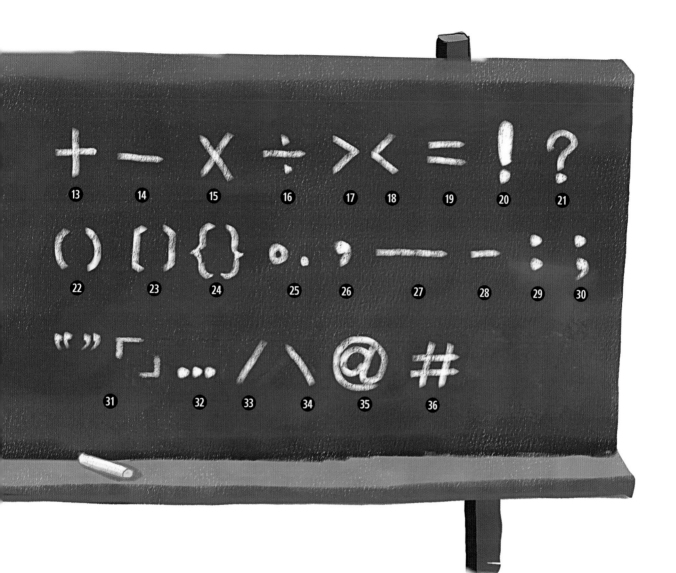

㉑ le point d'interrogation
question mark

㉒ les parenthèses parentheses

㉓ les crochets brackets

㉔ les accolades braces

㉕ le point period

㉖ la virgule comma

㉗ le tiret dash

㉘ le trait d'union hyphen

㉙ les deux points colon

㉚ le point-virgule semicolon

㉛ les guillemets quotation marks

㉜ les points de suspension ellipsis

㉝ le slash gauche slash

㉞ le slash droit backslash

㉟ l'arobase "at" symbol

㊱ dièse pound sign

❶ le saut en parachute skydiving

❷ le parapente hang gliding

❸ l'aviron boating

❹ le rafting white-water rafting

❺ la natation swimming

❻ le patinage artistique figure skating

❼ le patinage ice-skating

❽ le roller roller skating

❾ le patinage de vitesse speed skating

❿ le tir à l'arc archery

⑪ **le paintball** paintball

⑫ **les fléchettes** darts

⑬ **le jogging** jogging

⑭ **le cyclisme** cycling

⑮ **l'équitation** horseback riding

⑯ **la course automobile** car racing

⑰ **le skate** skateboarding

⑱ **faire du snowboard** snowboarding

⑲ **le ski** skiing

⑳ **l'escalade** rock climbing

❶ le bowling bowling

❷ le basketball basketball

❸ le handball handball

❹ le baseball baseball

❺ le dodgeball dodgeball

❻ le golf golf

❼ le tennis tennis

❽ le softball softball

❾ le tennis de table / le ping-pong
table tennis

⑩ le hockey sur glace ice hockey

⑪ le hockey sur gazon field hockey

⑫ le football soccer

⑬ le football américain
American football

⑭ le billard billiards

⑮ le volley volleyball

⑯ le badminton badminton

⑰ le cricket cricket

⑱ le squash squash

⑲ la pétanque boccie

❶ **la nage du chien** dog paddle

❷ **la brasse** breaststroke

❸ **le crawl** freestyle

❹ **le dos** backstroke

❺ **le papillon** butterfly stroke

❻ **la brasse indienne** sidestroke

❼ **le plongeon** diving

❽ **la natation synchronisée**
synchronized swimming

❾ le ski nautique waterskiing

❿ le surf surfing

⓫ le water-polo water polo

⓬ la planche à voile windsurfing

⓭ le jetski jet skiing

⓮ le snorkeling snorkeling

⓯ la plongée scuba diving

⓰ le parachute ascensionnel parasailing

❶ le lancer du marteau
hammer throw

❷ le lancer de disque
discus throw

❸ le lancer de poids shot put

❹ le saut en longueur long jump

❺ le saut en hauteur high jump

❻ le triple saut triple jump

❼ le saut de haies hurdles

❽ le saut à la perche pole vault

9 **le lancer de javelot** javelin throw

10 **la course d'obstacles** steeplechase

11 **le marathon** marathon

12 **la course de relais** relay race

13 **le sprint** sprint

14 **la marche athlétique** racewalking

15 **le 100 mètres** hundred-meter dash

❶ la souris mouse

❷ l'écureuil squirrel

❸ le kangourou kangaroo

❹ la chauve-souris bat

❺ le chien / la chienne dog

❻ le chat / la chatte cat

❼ le lapin / la lapine rabbit

❽ le porc / la truie pig

❾ le singe / la guenon monkey

❿ le koala koala

⓫ le bouc / la chèvre goat

⓬ le mouton / la brebis sheep

⓭ le taureau / la vache cow, bull

⓮ le cheval / la jument horse

⓯ le zèbre zebra

⑯ le chameau / la chamelle
camel

⑰ l'âne donkey

⑱ le cerf / la biche deer

⑲ la girafe giraffe

⑳ le loup / la louve wolf

㉑ le renard fox

㉒ le rhinocéros rhinoceros

㉓ l'hippopotame hippopotamus

㉔ le panda panda

㉕ l'ours bear

㉖ le lion / la lionne lion

㉗ le tigre / la tigresse tiger

㉘ l'éléphant elephant

㉙ l'ours polaire polar bear

❶ la mouche fly

❷ le moustique mosquito

❸ l'abeille bee

❹ la libellule dragonfly

❺ le papillon butterfly

❻ le papillon de nuit moth

❼ la cigale cicada

❽ le cafard cockroach

❾ le grillon cricket

❿ l'araignée spider

⓫ le scarabée scarab beetle, June bug

⓬ la coccinelle ladybug

⓭ la luciole firefly

⓮ le criquet grasshopper

⓯ la mante praying mantis

⑯ le scarabée rhinocéros japonais
rhinoceros beetle

⑰ la lucane stag beetle

⑱ l'escargot snail

⑲ la fourmi ant

⑳ le ver à soie silkworm

㉑ le ver de terre earthworm

㉒ le mille-pattes centipede

㉓ le scorpion scorpion

㉔ la puce flea

㉕ le têtard tadpole

㉖ la grenouille frog

㉗ le lézard lizard

㉘ le crocodile crocodile

㉙ le serpent snake

㉚ la tortue tortoise

❶ le coq / la poule chicken

❷ la dinde turkey

❸ le faisan pheasant

❹ le canard duck

❺ l'oie goose

❻ le cygne swan

❼ le pingouin penguin

❽ le goéland seagull

❾ l'aigrette blanche egret

❿ le pigeon pigeon

⓫ le moineau sparrow

⓬ le pic woodpecker

⓭ le canari canary

⓮ le corbeau crow

⓯ le martin huppé mynah

⑯ **le perroquet** parrot

⑰ **la pirolle de Taïwan** blue magpie

⑱ **le toucan** toucan

⑲ **le pélican** pelican

⑳ **l'alouette** lark

㉑ **le colibri** hummingbird

㉒ **l'hirondelle** swallow

㉓ **la pie-grièche** shrike

㉔ **le hibou** owl

㉕ **la petite spatule** spoonbill

㉖ **l'autruche** ostrich

㉗ **le paon** peacock

㉘ **l'aigle** eagle

㉙ **le vautour** vulture

㉚ **le condor** condor

❶ **le crabe** crab

❷ **la langouste** lobster

❸ **le fugu** blowfish

❹ **le dauphin** dolphin

❺ **le requin** shark

❻ **la baleine** whale

❼ **l'étoile de mer** starfish

❽ **le concombre de mer** sea cucumber

❾ **le serpent marin** sea snake

❿ **l'hippocampe** sea horse

⓫ **la méduse** jellyfish

⓬ **la tortue marine** sea turtle

⓭ **le phoque** seal

⓮ **le maquereau** mackerel

⑮ **la murène** moray (eel)

⑯ **la daurade** sea bream

⑰ **l'espadon** swordfish

⑱ **le poisson clown** clown fish

⑲ **la raie** stingray

⑳ **les poissons tropicaux / les poissons d'aquarium d'eau douce**
tropical fish

㉑ **le corail** coral

㉒ **l'algue** seaweed

㉓ **l'anémone de mer** sea anemone

㉔ **la conque** conch

㉕ **le poisson volant** flying fish

㉖ **le lamantin** manatee

㉗ **l'otarie** sea lion

❶ **le narcisse** narcissus

❷ **le rhododendron** azalea

❸ **le lys** lily

❹ **la marguerite** daisy

❺ **l'iris** iris

❻ **le camélia** camellia

❼ **la rose** rose

❽ **la fleur de cerisier / la sakura**
cherry blossom

❾ **l'œillet** carnation

❿ **l'ipomée** morning glory

⓫ **la lavande** lavender

⓬ **le tournesol** sunflower

⑬ la tulipe tulip

⑭ la giroflée violet

⑮ le colza canola

⑯ le pissenlit dandelion

⑰ le trèfle (à quatre feuilles) shamrock

⑱ l'orchidée orchid

⑲ la poinsettia poinsettia

⑳ la fougère fern

㉑ le saule willow

㉒ le pin pine tree

㉓ le cyprès cypress

㉔ l'érable maple

❶ janvier January

❷ février February

❸ mars March

❹ avril April

❺ mai May

❻ juin June

❼ juillet July

❽ août August

❾ septembre September

❿ octobre October

⓫ novembre November

⓬ décembre December

⓭ le calendrier paysan / le calendrier lunaire lunar calendar

⓮ l'année year

⓯ le mois month

⓰ le jour day

⑰ la date date

⑱ dimanche Sunday

⑲ lundi Monday

⑳ mardi Tuesday

㉑ mercredi Wednesday

㉒ jeudi Thursday

㉓ vendredi Friday

㉔ samedi Saturday

㉕ avant-hier the day before yesterday

㉖ hier yesterday

㉗ aujourd'hui today

㉘ demain tomorrow

㉙ après-demain the day after tomorrow

㉚ la fête nationale / le jour férié
national holiday

㉛ le temps time

㉜ l'heure hour

㉝ la minute minute

㉞ la seconde second

❶ le soleil sun

❷ le nuage cloud

❸ la pluie rain

❹ le vent wind

❺ le tonnerre thunder

❻ l'éclair lightning

❼ le brouillard fog

❽ le gel frost

❾ la neige snow

❿ la glace ice

⓫ la grêle hail

⓬ la tempête storm

⑬ **l'ouragan** hurricane

⑭ **la tornade** tornado

⑮ **la dépression** low pressure

⑯ **l'anticyclone** high pressure

⑰ **le front froid** cold front

⑱ **la vague de froid** cold current

⑲ **la température** temperature

⑳ **le printemps** spring

㉑ **l'été** summer

㉒ **l'automne** fall, autumn

㉓ **l'hiver** winter

㉔ **dégagé** sunny day

㉕ **couvert** cloudy day

㉖ **pluvieux** rainy day

❶ le Jour de l'an New Year

❷ le réveillon de la Saint-Sylvestre
New Year's Eve

❸ la Saint-Valentin Valentine's Day

❹ Pâques Easter

❺ le Jeudi de l'Ascension
Feast of the Ascension

❻ la Fête du travail Labor Day

❼ la Fête nationale Bastille Day

❽ l'Assomption the Assumption

❾ la Toussaint All Saints' Day

❿ Noël Christmas

⓫ la fête des mères Mother's Day

⓬ la fête des pères Father's Day

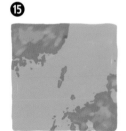   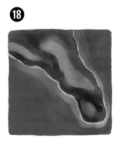 

❶ le plateau plateau

❷ la forêt forest

❸ le lac lake

❹ la cascade waterfall

❺ la rivière river

❻ l'étang pond

❼ la montagne mountain

❽ la vallée valley

❾ le bassin basin

❿ la plaine plain

⓫ le banc de sable sandbar

⓬ la plage beach

⓭ l'océan ocean, sea

⓮ l'île island

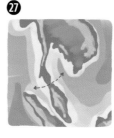

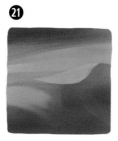

⑮ le détroit strait

⑯ l'archipel archipelago

⑰ la barrière de corail coral reef

⑱ la péninsule peninsula

⑲ la baie bay

⑳ le désert desert

㉑ la dune dune

㉒ le glacier glacier

㉓ la colline hills

㉔ le marais bog, swamp

㉕ le fjord fjord

㉖ le volcan volcano

㉗ l'isthme isthmus

㉘ la forêt tropicale rainforest

Index

information desk 79, 87
ink 103
institute of continuing education 95
insurance counter 86
internal medicine specialist 92
intersection 83
intestines 35
iris 124
iron 18
iron the clothes 24
ironing board 18
island 132
isthmus 133

kiwi fruit 42
kneel 38
knit 24
koala 116

L

lab 97
Labor Day 130
laborer 31
ladder 23
ladle 20
ladybug 118
lake 132
lamb 46
lamp 17
landing 86
language class 95
language lab 96
laptop computer 8
lark 121
lasagna 56
laugh 37
laundry bag 19
laundry basket 13
laundry detergent 18
lavatory 84
lavender 124
law 98
lawyer 32
LCD monitor 8
leather goods department 79
leather shoes 68
leg of lamb 46
lemon 42
lemonade 50
less than 106
letter 72
letter carrier 72
lettuce 45
library 97
lie down 39
lie facedown 39

life preserver 84
light 104
light bulb 6
lightning 128
lily 124
lingerie department 78
linguistics 98
lion 117
lipstick 15
listen to music 89
literature 98
liver 35
lizard 119
loach 48
lobster 122
lockers 79, 97
long jump 114
lost-and-found department 78
low-fat milk 51
low pressure 129
luggage 86
luggage carousel 87
luggage cart 86
lunar calendar 126
lung 35

M

mackerel 122
mailbox 3, 72
main door 2
man 26
manager 30
manatee 123
mango 42
map 101
maple 125
marathon 115
March 126
marinate 61
maritime mail 73
marker 102
mascara 14

mask 15
master's degree 95
math 98
mattress 17
May 126
meat 40
meatballs 47
mechanic 31
mechanical pencil 102
medicine 98
melon 42
membership card 40
men's department 79
menu 54
microphone 101
microwave food 40
microwave oven 20
middle-aged person 26
midterm 99
milk shake 51
mineral water 50
minus 106
minute 127
mirror 11
modem 8
moisturizer 14
Monday 127
money order 77
monkey 116
monorail 80
month 126
monthly test 99
mop 19
moray 123
morning glory 124
mosquito 118
moth 118
mother 28
mother-in-law 29
Mother's Day 131
motherboard 8
motorboat 80
motorcycle 81

mountain 132
mountain climbing 88
mouse 8, 116
mouse pad 8
mouth 35
movie theater 71
muffins 53
mug 59
multiplication 106
mushroom 45
music 98
musician 33
mustard 63
mynah 120

N

nail 22
nail clipper 13
nail polish 15
napkin 55
narcissus 124
national holiday 127
navel 35
neck 35
necklace 67
necktie 67
nephew 29
nervous 37
network adapter card 8
New Year 130
New Year's Eve 130
niece 29
nightclub 71
nightstand 17
non-fat milk 51
nose 35
notebook 103
November 126
nurse 32, 93
nurse's office 97
nurses' station 93

Index

Index